# SUMMER MATH WORKBOOK

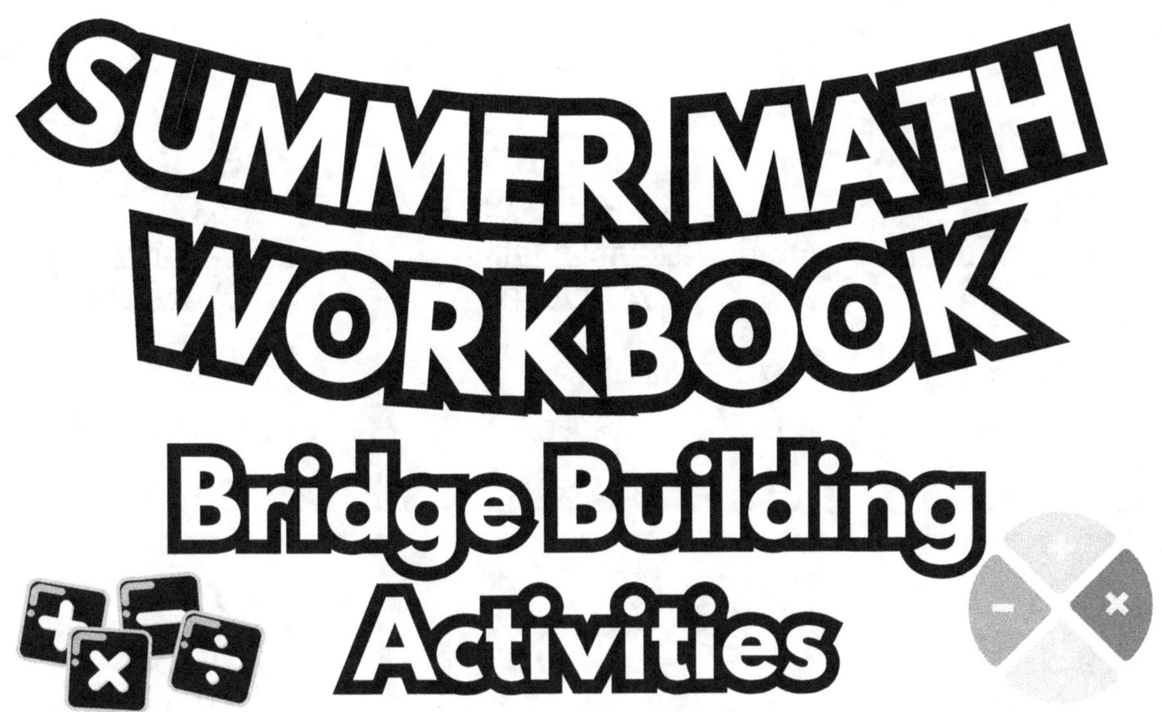

Grade
1 2
SUMMER MATH WORKBOOK
Bridge Building Activities
Number Sense
Addition and Subtraction
Place Value

Grade
2 3
SUMMER MATH WORKBOOK
Bridge Building Activities
Number Sense
Addition and Subtraction
Place Value

Grade
3 4
SUMMER MATH WORKBOOK
Bridge Building Activities
Number Sense
Addition and Subtraction
Place Value

Grade
4 5
SUMMER MATH WORKBOOK
Bridge Building Activities
Multiplication and Division
Place Value and Units
Fractions and Geometry



Grade
5 6
SUMMER MATH WORKBOOK
Bridge Building Activities
Multiplication and Division
Factors and Multiples
Fractions and Geometry

Grade
6 7
SUMMER MATH WORKBOOK
Bridge Building Activities
Arithmetic
Algebra
Geometry and Statistics



Grade
7 8
SUMMER MATH WORKBOOK
Bridge Building Activities
Ratio and Percentage
Algebra and Cartesian Plane
Geometry and Statistics



Grade
8 9
SUMMER MATH WORKBOOK
Bridge Building Activities
Ratio and Percentage
Algebra
Geometry and Graphing



Grade
9 10
SUMMER MATH WORKBOOK
Bridge Building Activities
Factoring and Distributing
Algebra
Geometry and Graphing

# Introduction

As parents and educators, we understand the pivotal role that mathematics plays in shaping a child's academic journey and future success. Yet, the path to mathematical proficiency can often seem daunting, filled with challenges and complexities. That's where the transformative power of Summer Bridge Building Activities books comes into play, illuminating the way forward with clarity, precision, and purpose.

Summer vacation is a time for rest and relaxation, but it also presents the risk of the "summer slide," where students lose some of the academic gains they made during the school year. Summer Bridge Building Activities books are specifically designed to tackle this challenge, ensuring that your child stays academically engaged and prepared for the upcoming school year. These books provide a seamless bridge from one grade to the next, reinforcing essential skills and introducing new concepts that will give your child a head start.

Imagine your child eagerly diving into the pages of a Summer Bridge Building Activities book, greeted by clear, engaging content that demystifies complex mathematical concepts. With each turn of the pages, they embark on a journey of discovery, encountering thoughtfully curated practice questions that reinforce learning and sharpen problem-solving skills. As they unveil the answers to those questions, a sense of accomplishment blossoms within them — a tangible reward for their hard work and dedication.

Summer Bridge Building Activities books transcend traditional educational tools; they are meticulously crafted to build a deep and enduring understanding of mathematics. These books follow a sequential and logical progression, starting from fundamental principles and advancing to sophisticated problem-solving strategies. Each chapter is designed to build on the previous one, ensuring a solid and comprehensive foundation for future learning.

Parents, we yearn for nothing more than to see our children thrive academically and personally. We want to witness the spark of inspiration ignited within them as they overcome academic challenges with confidence and poise. Summer Bridge Building Activities books serve as indispensable partners in this noble endeavor, offering not just practice questions but the keys to unlocking a world of academic and personal opportunities.

Visualize the pride on your child's face as they master a challenging math concept, the joy they experience when their efforts yield results, and the confidence they gain with each success. These pages are designed to make learning math a positive, enriching, and deeply rewarding experience that will benefit them throughout their academic journey and beyond.

For educators, Summer Bridge Building Activities books are invaluable allies in the quest to cultivate mathematical proficiency in the classroom. Accompanied by comprehensive guides and readily available answers, instructors can focus on mentoring and nurturing their students, secure in the knowledge that these books provide a robust framework for effective learning.

Within the pages of Summer Bridge Building Activities books lies not just the promise of academic excellence, but the seeds of a brighter future. By integrating these resources into your child's summer routine, you are bestowing upon them the gifts of confidence, curiosity, and a lifelong love of learning.

Invest in your child's future today with Summer Bridge Building Activities books — because every great journey begins with a single step, and this step can change everything. Keep the momentum of learning alive over the summer, and watch your child soar to new academic heights.

# Contents

Grade 7-9
PRE ALGEBRA WORKBOOK
BRIDGE BUILDING ACTIVITIES
Equations, Inequalities and Expressions
Linear Equations Graphing and Slope
System of Equations Quadratic Equations

Grade 6-8
PRE ALGEBRA WORKBOOK
BRIDGE BUILDING ACTIVITIES
Equations One Side and Two Sides
Verbal Algebra Expressions
Linear Equations and Slope Order of Operations

Grade 5-6
PRE ALGEBRA WORKBOOK
BRIDGE BUILDING ACTIVITIES
Integers, Mixed Numbers Decimals and Fractions
Place Value Exponents and Roots
Percentage and Ratio Word Problems

PRE ALGEBRA WORKBOOK
for Beginners
Integers Fractions, Mixed Numbers
Place Value Exponents and Roots
Percentage Ratio Conversion

PRE ALGEBRA WORKBOOK
for Adults
Integers Percent and Ratio
Equations, Inequalities Expressions
Order of Operations


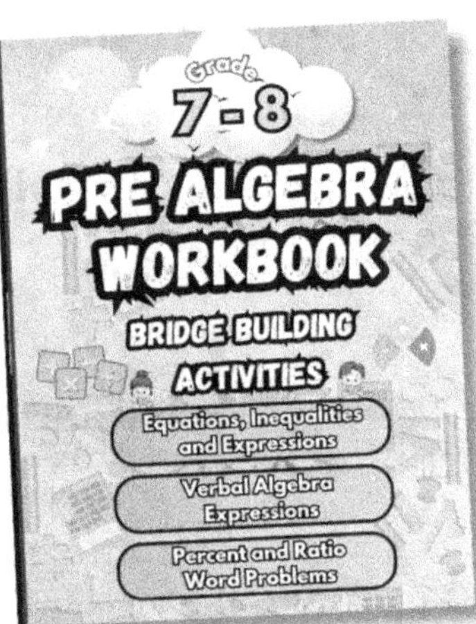

Grade 7-8
PRE ALGEBRA WORKBOOK
BRIDGE BUILDING ACTIVITIES
Equations, Inequalities and Expressions
Verbal Algebra Expressions
Percent and Ratio Word Problems


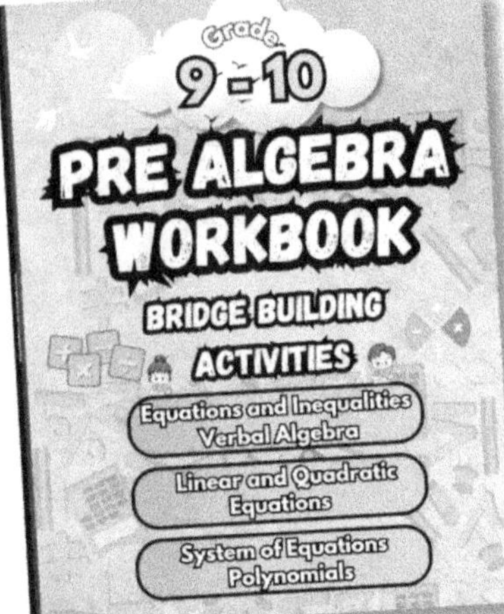

Grade 9-10
PRE ALGEBRA WORKBOOK
BRIDGE BUILDING ACTIVITIES
Equations and Inequalities Verbal Algebra
Linear and Quadratic Equations
System of Equations Polynomials

Grade 8th
ALGEBRA 1 WORKBOOK
BRIDGE BUILDING ACTIVITIES
Order of Operations
One and Two Step Equations and Expressions
Linear Equations Cartesian Plane

Grade 7-9
ALGEBRA 1 WORKBOOK
BRIDGE BUILDING ACTIVITIES
Integers Order of Operations
One and Multi Step Equations and Expressions
Linear, Quadratic Equations Equations One Side, Two Sides

<u>**Solving Equations (One Side)**</u>

Solving one-step equations involves performing a single operation to isolate the variable and find its value.

Let's solve an equation step by step: $16 + x = 31$

1. Identify the Goal:

   The goal is to isolate the variable $x$ on one side of the equation.

2. Simplify the Equation: Combine like terms on both sides of the equation, if necessary.

   The equation is already simplified.

3. Undo Addition or Subtraction: If there's addition or subtraction involving the variable, undo it by performing the opposite operation on both sides of the equation.

   Since $x$ is being added to 16, we'll undo this operation by subtracting 16 from both sides of the equation:

   $$16 + x - 16 = 31 - 16$$

4. Isolate the Variable: Ensure that the variable is alone on one side of the equation.

   $$x = 15$$

5. Check Your Solution: Substitute the value of $x$ back into the original equation to verify that it satisfies the equation.

   $$16 + 15 = 31$$

   $$31 = 31$$

The equation is balanced.

## Equations (One Side)

Solve for the variable.

1) $x - 3 = 4$

2) $y + 10 = 15$

3) $z \times 2 = 10$

4) $1y + 3 = 10$

5) $1y + 3 = 12$

6) $y + 8 = 14$

7) $y - 1 = 8$

8) $1 - z = 0$

9) $8 + 7k = 57$

10) $z + 1 = 3$

11) $9 \times x = 36$

12) $y \div 4 = 4$

13) $5y - 2 = 8$

14) $9 + z = 12$

15) $3 - m = 2$

16) $z + 9 = 18$

17) $1m + 2 = 12$

18) $6 + 2y = 8$

19) $9 + 6x = 21$

20) $14 - 1m = 6$

**21)** $8x - 10 = 46$

**22)** $1m + 4 = 13$

**23)** $58 - 6x = 4$

**24)** $7 - k = 2$

**25)** $5 - y = 4$

**26)** $9 \div x = 1$

**27)** $82 - 10y = 2$

**28)** $24 \div z = 6$

**29)** $5 + 9y = 23$

**30)** $9 \times y = 54$

31) $z + 1 = 11$

32) $m \div 2 = 4$

33) $8 - 4k = 4$

34) $k + 8 = 11$

35) $10 - m = 4$

36) $m + 2 = 9$

37) $y + 2 = 3$

38) $74 - 7y = 4$

39) $k \times 5 = 15$

40) $10 - z = 7$

41) $k + 8 = 10$

42) $6 + x = 8$

43) $8 \times k = 64$

44) $m \div 4 = 6$

45) $7 \times m = 49$

46) $1y - 1 = 7$

47) $9 + 10y = 79$

48) $7z - 5 = 44$

49) $m \times 10 = 10$

50) $30 - 6z = 6$

**51)** $42 \div y = 6$

**52)** $10 - 1y = 1$

**53)** $6 \times k = 54$

**54)** $m \times 4 = 28$

**55)** $5y - 7 = 43$

**56)** $8 - k = 3$

**57)** $7 + m = 16$

**58)** $6 - z = 1$

**59)** $8 \div z = 4$

**60)** $m + 3 = 8$

**61)** $5 + z = 10$

**62)** $73 - 8z = 9$

**63)** $k - 2 = 1$

**64)** $6 + x = 9$

**65)** $k \div 7 = 8$

**66)** $m \div 5 = 4$

**67)** $49 - 6x = 1$

**68)** $x - 8 = 2$

**69)** $8 + x = 13$

**70)** $7 \times z = 42$

## Equations (Two Sides)

A two-sided equation is an equation where both sides have expressions with variables and constants. The goal when solving a two-sided equation is to find the value of the variable that makes both sides equal.

For example: Let's solve an equation:

$$9 + 8x + 8 = 64 + x + 2$$

- Combine Like Terms: Simplify each side of the equation by combining like terms (terms with the same variable or constants).

$$9 + 8x + 8 = 64 + x + 2$$
$$17 + 8x = 66 + x$$

- Isolate the Variable: Use inverse operations to isolate the variable on one side of the equation.

subtract x from both sides:

$$17 + 8x - x = 66 + x - x$$
$$17 + 7x = 66$$

subtracting 17 from both sides:

$$17 - 17 + 7x = 66 - 17$$
$$7x = 49$$

divide both sides by 7:

$$\frac{7x}{7} = \frac{49}{7} = x = 7$$

- Check Solution: Once you find the solution, substitute it back into the original equation to ensure it makes the equation true.

Substitute $x = 7$ back into the original equation:

$$9 + 8(7) + 8 = 64 + 7 + 2$$
$$9 + 56 + 8 = 64 + 7 + 2$$
$$73 = 73$$

## Equations (Two Sides)

Solve for the variable.

**1)** $6 + 5x = 38 + x$

**2)** $23 + y = 4y + 2$

**3)** $5 + 8z = 41 - z$

**4)** $57 - z = 8z + 3$

**5)** $8k = 56 + k$

**6)** $3m + 5 = 37 - m$

**7)** $3 + 7z = 11 - z$

**8)** $35 + z = 6z$

**9)** $8 + 6y = 29 - y$

**10)** $11 + k = 9 + 3k$

**11)** $6y = 42 - y$

**12)** $3k = 8 + k$

**13)** $17 + y = 3y + 5$

**14)** $6 + 8z = 51 - z$

**15)** $9 + m = 2m$

**16)** $22 - m = 7 + 4m$

**17)** $3y = 20 - y$

**18)** $25 + z = 6z$

**19)** $4 - m = 3m$

**20)** $1 + 5x = 21 + x$

**21)** $4 + 3z = 12 + z$

**22)** $7 - x = 4 + 2x$

**23)** $4z + 2 = 12 - z$

**24)** $7y = 48 + y$

**25)** $35 + m = 8m$

**26)** $10 + z = 1 + 4z$

**27)** $13 + k = 4 + 2k$

**28)** $16 - k = 7k$

**29)** $5 + 2x = 20 - x$

**30)** $2y = 27 - y$

**31)** $32 + y = 5y + 4$

**32)** $38 + m = 6m + 8$

**33)** $5x + 3 = 15 - x$

**34)** $3m + 5 = 17 - m$

**35)** $11 + m = 7 + 2m$

**36)** $6y + 4 = 14 + y$

**37)** $8 - x = 6x + 1$

**38)** $2m = 21 - m$

**39)** $11 - y = 2y + 2$

**40)** $28 - y = 6y$

**41)** $9 + 3x = 41 - x$

**42)** $3z + 8 = 12 + z$

**43)** $9 - z = 2z$

**44)** $12 + z = 8z + 5$

**45)** $4z = 10 - z$

**46)** $7 + 6k = 42 - k$

**47)** $34 + x = 6x + 4$

**48)** $5y = 32 + y$

**49)** $6 + z = 2z + 3$

**50)** $3z = 2 + z$

**51)** $2z = 1 + z$

**52)** $18 - y = 2y$

**53)** $16 - m = 3m$

**54)** $8 + 7k = 32 + k$

**55)** $4y + 8 = 23 + y$

**56)** $3k = 28 - k$

**57)** $8 - y = 7y$

**58)** $2 + k = 2k$

**59)**  $8y = 72 - y$

**60)**  $23 + m = 9 + 8m$

**61)**  $18 - m = 2m$

**62)**  $3z + 9 = 25 - z$

**63)**  $2 + 4x = 14 + x$

**64)**  $2z + 9 = 16 + z$

**65)**  $57 - x = 5x + 3$

**66)**  $29 + x = 8 + 4x$

**67)**  $4x = 24 + x$

**68)**  $3x = 12 + x$

**69)** $2x + 7 = 28 - x$

**70)** $24 - y = 7y$

**71)** $1 + 2y = 10 + y$

**72)** $3 + x = 1 + 2x$

**73)** $8 + 8m = 71 + m$

**74)** $18 + y = 3y + 6$

**75)** $2k + 5 = 14 + k$

**76)** $16 - k = 3k + 4$

**77)** $3y + 7 = 25 + y$

**78)** $42 - k = 5k$

<u>**Order of Operations (PEMDAS)**</u>

The order of operations, often remembered by the acronym PEMDAS, stands for:

- **Parentheses**: Perform operations inside parentheses first.
- **Exponents**: Evaluate exponents (powers and roots) next.
- **Multiplication and Division**: Perform multiplication and division from left to right.
- **Addition and Subtraction:** Perform addition and subtraction from left to right.

The order of operations helps to clarify which operations should be performed first in a mathematical expression to ensure consistent and accurate results.

- **Parentheses**: Evaluate expressions within parentheses first. If there are nested parentheses, start with the innermost ones and work your way out.

   1. Example: $2 \times ( 3 + 4) = 2 \times 7 = 14$

- **Exponents**: Evaluate expressions with exponents (powers and roots) next.

   1. Example: $2^3 + 4 = 8 + 4 = 12$

- **Multiplication and Division**: Perform multiplication and division from left to right.

   1. Example: $2 \times 3 + 4 = 6 + 4 = 10$

   2. Example: $6 \div 2 \times 3 = 3 \times 3 = 9$

- **Addition and Subtraction**: Perform addition and subtraction from left to right.

   1. Example: $2 + 3 \times 4 = 2 + 12 = 14$

   2. Example: $10 - 4 \div 2 = 10 - 2 = 8$

## Order of Operations (PEMDAS)

Evaluate Expressions.

**1)** $(3 \times 1) - (7 + 9) =$

**2)** $6 + 9 + 6 + 4 =$

**3)** $(1 + 3)(1 + 5) =$

**4)** $(9 + 9) \times (7 + 6) =$

**5)** $(4 + 4) \times (8 + 7) =$

**6)** $(4^2) \times (10^2) + 1 =$

**7)** $(3 + 1)^2 + (5 + 3)^2 =$

**8)** $(10 + 1) \times (6 + 5) =$

9) $(2 + 1) \times (9 + 3) =$

10) $(2 + 4) \times (2 + 2) =$

11) $(10 \times 7) - (7 + 2) =$

12) $7 \times 8 + 7 =$

13) $(2^2) \times (9^2) + 2 =$

14) $(5 + 10)^2 =$

15) $1 + 3 - 5 + 3 =$

16) $3(1 + 4) =$

17) $9(1 + 7) =$

18) $6 \times 3 \times 6 =$

**19)** $(9 + 9)(4 + 10) =$

**20)** $(6 + 6) \times (2 + 3) =$

**21)** $3 \times 9 \times 1 =$

**22)** $7 + 8^2 =$

**23)** $4 \times 5 + 5 =$

**24)** $4 \times 4 \times 9 =$

**25)** $6 + 7 - 5 + 9 =$

**26)** $7 \times 6 =$

**27)** $(10 + 1) \div 1 =$

**28)** $3 + 1^2 =$

**29)** $3 \times 1 + 4 =$

**30)** $(6 \times 8) - (9 + 4) =$

**31)** $2 \times 3 \times 6 =$

**32)** $4 \times 7 + 8 =$

**33)** $5 + 4 + 7 =$

**34)** $5 + 8^2 =$

**35)** $(9 + 4)^2 =$

**36)** $(7^2) \times (3^2) + 7 =$

**37)** $(8 + 10) \times (5 + 1) =$

**38)** $(7 \times 5) - (6 + 6) =$

**39)** $(2 + 10)(2 + 6) =$

**40)** $10 \times 3 =$

**41)** $3 + 6 + 6 =$

**42)** $2 \times 3 + 2 =$

**43)** $4 + 3 - 10 + 7 =$

**44)** $5 + 3 + 10 =$

**45)** $5 + 3^2 + 2 + 10^2 =$

**46)** $(5 \times 1) - (5 + 7) =$

**47)** $7 + 4 + 9 + 7 =$

**48)** $7 + 7 + 1 =$

49) $2 + 8 + 7 + 9 =$

50) $5(4 + 3) =$

51) $(3 + 3)(3 + 4) =$

52) $2 + 4^2 =$

53) $5 + 1 + 8 + 6 =$

54) $4 + 5^2 =$

55) $1 + 3 + 1 =$

56) $10 + 8 + 5 =$

57) $(5^2) \times (7^2) + 6 =$

58) $2 \times 8 + 5 =$

**59)** $6 + 5 + 3 =$

**60)** $(2^2) \times (2^2) + 1 =$

**61)** $7 \times 8 \times 6 =$

**62)** $3 + 1 - 9 + 8 =$

**63)** $1 + 10 + 2 + 2 =$

**64)** $7 \times 6 + 3 =$

**65)** $3 + 2^2 =$

**66)** $6 + 8 - 2 + 8 =$

**67)** $10 + 4 + 1 + 8 =$

**68)** $(7 + 1)^2 =$

# Mixed Numbers: Addition and Subtraction

To add or subtract mixed numbers, we follow similar steps as when adding or subtracting regular fractions. For instance:

## Addition:

- Add the whole numbers: Add the whole number parts of the mixed numbers together.
- Add the fractions: Add the fractions parts of the mixed numbers together.
- Simplify (if needed): If the fraction part of the sum is an improper fraction, simplify it by converting it to a mixed number.

## Subtraction:

- Subtract the whole numbers: Subtract the whole number part of the second mixed number from the whole number part of the first mixed number.
- Subtract the fractions: Subtract the fraction part of the second mixed number from the fraction part of the first mixed number.
- Simplify (if needed): If the fraction part of the difference is a negative fraction, borrow from the whole number part or simplify it by converting it to a mixed number.

# Mixed Numbers: Multiplication and Division

To multiply or divide mixed numbers, we follow these steps:

## Multiplication:

- Convert the mixed numbers to improper fractions: Multiply the whole number by the denominator of the fraction, then add the numerator. Write the result over the original denominator.
- Multiply the fractions: Multiply the numerators together to get the new numerator and multiply the denominators together to get the new denominator.
- Simplify (if needed): If the result is an improper fraction, simplify it by converting it back to a mixed number.

## Division:

- Convert the mixed numbers to improper fractions:
- Invert the divisor: Flip the second fraction (the one you're dividing by) so that the division becomes multiplication.
- Multiply the fractions: Multiply the numerators together to get the new numerator and multiply the denominators together to get the new denominator.
- Simplify (if needed): If the result is an improper fraction, simplify it by converting it back to a mixed number.

## Mixed Numbers

Calculate.

**1)** $9\frac{1}{6} + 7\frac{3}{4} =$

**2)** $5\frac{1}{2} \div 9\frac{3}{5} =$

**3)** $9\frac{2}{3} - 8\frac{7}{9} =$

**4)** $1\frac{3}{8} \div 1\frac{4}{10} =$

**5)** $7\frac{3}{5} \times 5\frac{3}{4} =$

**6)** $9\frac{5}{9} + 2\frac{3}{8} =$ ________________________

**7)** $3\frac{1}{3} \div 3\frac{4}{10} =$ ________________________

**8)** $5\frac{1}{2} \div 8\frac{3}{6} =$ ________________________

**9)** $8\frac{6}{7} \div 8\frac{5}{7} =$ ________________________

**10)** $8\frac{1}{2} - 7\frac{2}{6} =$ ________________________

11) $6\frac{3}{9} + 6\frac{4}{5} =$ _______________

12) $6\frac{1}{3} + 4\frac{6}{10} =$ _______________

13) $6\frac{6}{8} - 5\frac{3}{4} =$ _______________

14) $5\frac{7}{9} \times 9\frac{6}{7} =$ _______________

15) $1\frac{1}{3} + 7\frac{1}{4} =$ _______________

**16)** $7\frac{2}{6} + 5\frac{1}{5} =$ _______________

**17)** $5\frac{1}{2} - 4\frac{3}{10} =$ _______________

**18)** $6\frac{5}{8} - 2\frac{2}{8} =$ _______________

**19)** $5\frac{1}{4} - 3\frac{4}{9} =$ _______________

**20)** $8\frac{6}{7} \times 8\frac{4}{5} =$ _______________

## Solving Inequalities

Inequalities are mathematical expressions that compare the relative sizes of two values. They are used to express relationships where one quantity is:

- "$<$" (less than),
- "$>$" (greater than),
- "$<=$" (less than or equal to),
- "$>=$" (greater than or equal to),
- and "$\neq$" (not equal to) another quantity.

For example:

$$y + \text{-}10 \leq -8$$

To isolate $y$, we need to get rid of the constant term $-10$. Since $-10$ is being subtracted from $y$, we can undo this operation by adding 10 to both sides of the inequality:

$$y - 10 + 10 \leq -8 + 10$$

$$y \leq 2$$

To check the solution:

$$2 - 10 \leq -8$$

$$-8 = -8$$

The inequality is true when $y = 2$

# SUMMER ALGEBRA WORKBOOK

### BUILDING ACTIVITIES

## Solving Inequalities

**1)**

$$-9 \leq x + -8$$

**2)**

$$\frac{y}{7} < -9$$

**3)**

$$7 > m - -8$$

**4)**

$$-3 > 5\,m$$

5)
$z - {-1} \geq 0$

6)

$-8 + x > 5$

7)
$-8z \geq -6$

8)
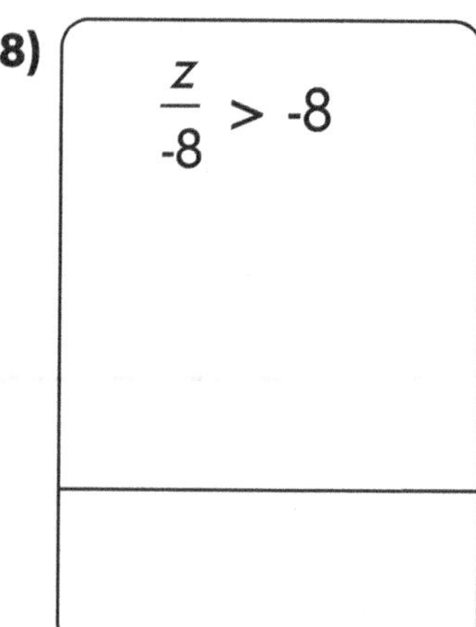
$\dfrac{z}{-8} > -8$

9)

$$16\,m \leq -8$$

10)

$$-2 - k < 7$$

11)

$$x + 1 > 1$$

12)

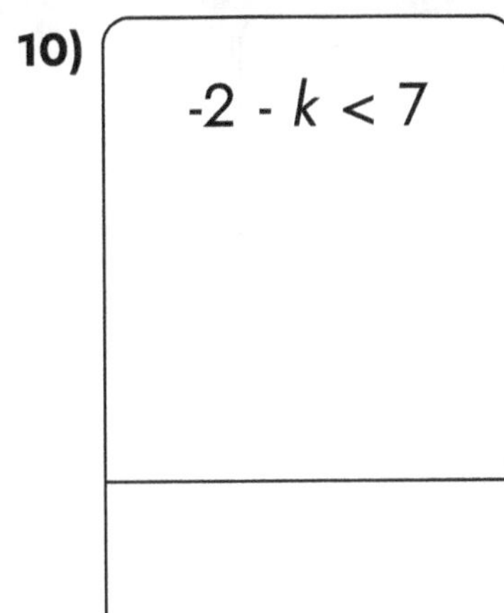

$$3 > \frac{z}{-8}$$

13)
$$\frac{k}{2} > 6$$

14)
$$-5 > m + -1$$

15)
$$1 \geq -2 - x$$

16)
$$12\,k < -20$$

17)

$$\frac{m}{-4} \le -5$$

18)

$$k + -3 > -5$$

19)

$$-8 - y \ge -6$$

20)

$$-3 \le -2\,m$$

21)

$$-1 \leq -3 - z$$

22) 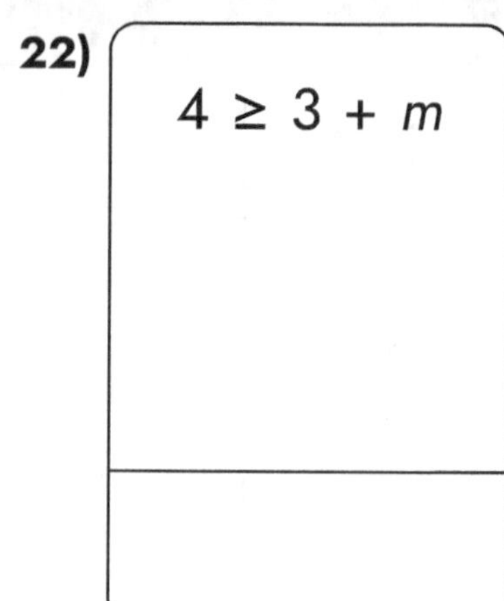

$$4 \geq 3 + m$$

23)

$$8 < -8\,y$$

24) 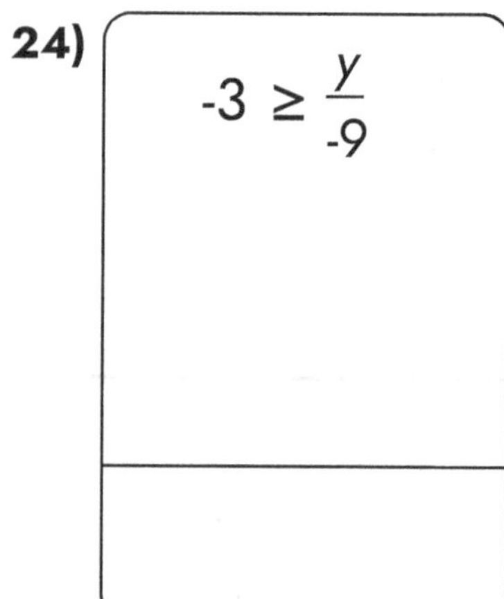

$$-3 \geq \frac{y}{-9}$$

**25)**

$$7 \geq z - {-4}$$

**26)**

$$-4 \leq 2 + m$$

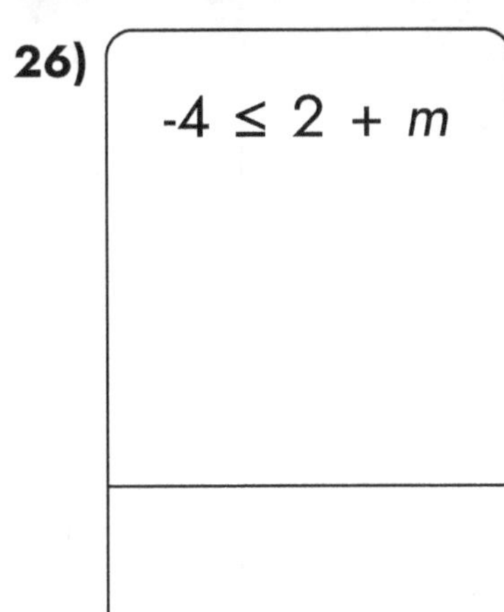

**27)**

$$-2x > 5$$

**28)**

$$\frac{z}{-1} < 7$$

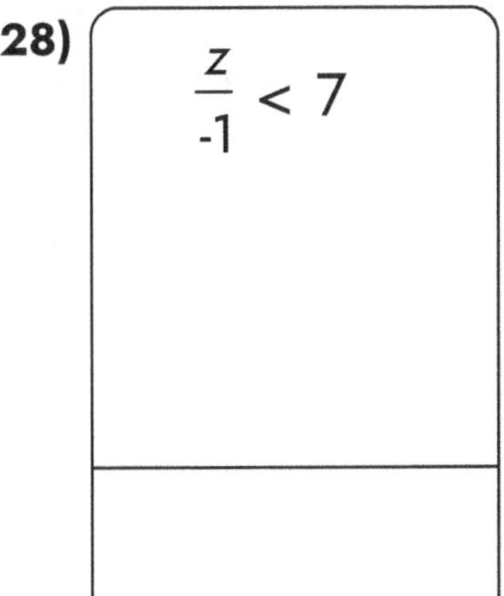

29)

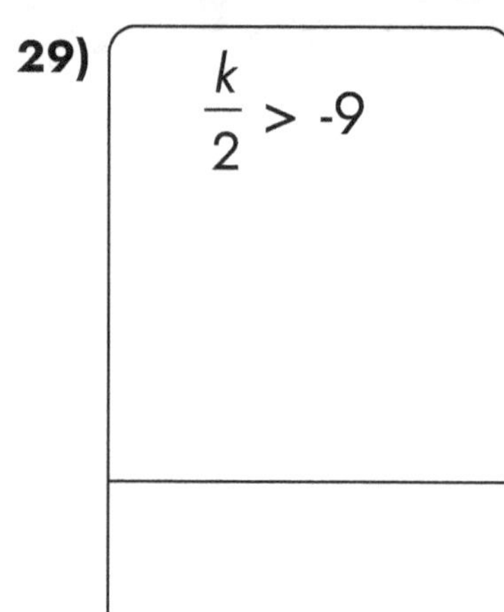

$$\frac{k}{2} > -9$$

30)

$$6 < x - -7$$

31)

$$-5 < -3x$$

32)

$$y + -1 \geq -4$$

**33)** $\dfrac{m}{-7} > 5$

**34)** $m + \text{-}6 \leq 9$

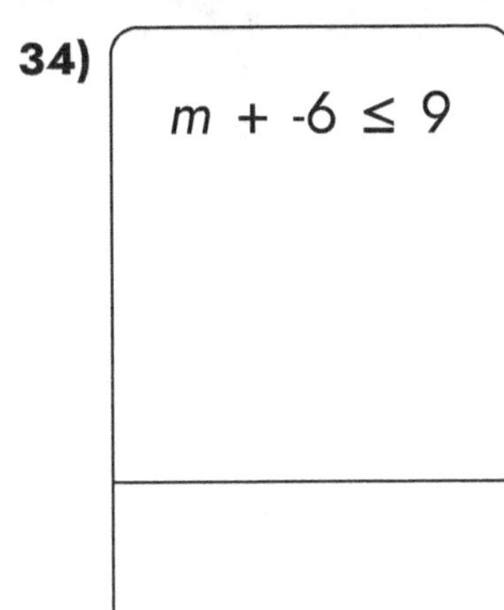

**35)** $4 \leq x - 2$

**36)** $4 \leq 2m$

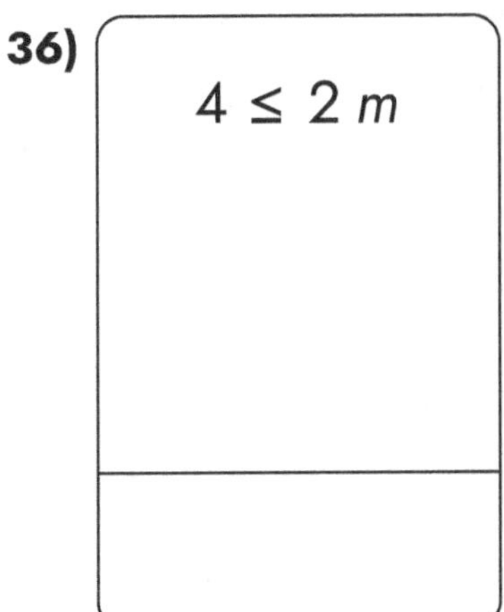

**37)**

$$\frac{x}{-7} > 2$$

**38)**

$$15\,m < 18$$

**39)**

$$9 \le 5 + m$$

**40)**

$$-9 - y \le 7$$

**41)**

$$4 \leq x + {-3}$$

**42)**

$$6 \leq -14\,y$$

**43)**

$$7 \geq k - 5$$

**44)**

$$\frac{k}{8} > 7$$

45)

$$0 \geq -6 - y$$

46)

$$\frac{z}{-5} \leq -8$$

47)

$$6 \leq -7 + y$$

48)

$$6 \geq 4x$$

<u>**Solving Equations**</u>

Evaluating expressions involves substituting given values for variables in an expression and then performing the indicated operations to find the result.

For example: Let's evaluate  $4x - 10$, when $x = 3$:

**Step 1: Substitute the given value for the variable:**

Replace every occurrence of x in the expression $4x - 10$ with the given value, which is 3:

$$= 4(3) - 10$$

**Step 2: Perform the operations:**

Perform the indicated operations according to the order of operations (PEMDAS - Parentheses, Exponents, Multiplication and Division, Addition and Subtraction):

$$= 4 \times 3 - 10$$

**Step 3: Simplify:**

Calculate the result:

$$12 - 10 = 2$$

## Solving Equations

Evaluate each expression when: x = 3

**1)** $x + 7 =$

**2)** $(x + 1) + (8x - 8) =$

**3)** $8x + 6 =$

**4)** $7^1 + x^1 =$

**5)** $7(8 - x) =$

**6)** $2x + 5 =$

**7)** $10x + 7 =$

**8)** $2x - 9 =$

**9)** $3x + 3 =$

**10)** $x + 6 =$

## Solving Equations

Evaluate each expression when: $x = 7$

**1)** $5x + 3x + x =$

**2)** $10x - 8 + 6x =$

**3)** $5x - 9 =$

**4)** $4 + (4x + 1) =$

**5)** $3x + x =$

**6)** $2(8 + x) =$

**7)** $7 \div x =$

**8)** $3x - 7 + 8x =$

**9)** $x + 7 + 5x =$

**10)** $2 + 9x =$

## Solving Equations

Evaluate each expression when: $x = 5$

**1)** $(7x)(4x) =$

**2)** $9x + x =$

**3)** $5(1 + x) =$

**4)** $10 + (6x + 4) - 4 + (9x) =$

**5)** $2(2 + x) =$

**6)** $8x - 4 =$

**7)** $3x + 5 =$

**8)** $(10x)(3x) =$

**9)** $(4x)(3x) =$

**10)** $x + 6 =$

## Solving Equations

Evaluate each expression when: $x = 6$

**1)** $4x - 7 =$

**2)** $5x + 5x + 8x =$

**3)** $x - 9 =$

**4)** $7 + (8x + 2) =$

**5)** $x^1 + 9x^1 =$

**6)** $10x + 2 =$

**7)** $3x + 5 =$

**8)** $8x + 9 - 6x =$

**9)** $\dfrac{x}{2} + 5 =$

**10)** $x - 7 =$

## Solving Equations

Evaluate each expression when: $x = 7$

**1)** $10x - x =$

**2)** $5x - x =$

**3)** $5 + x =$

**4)** $9 \div (x + 2) =$

**5)** $x + 10 =$

**6)** $8x + 7 =$

**7)** $2(7 - x) =$

**8)** $\dfrac{21}{x} =$

**9)** $6(2x - 6) + 10(7 + x) =$

**10)** $8 + (4x + 2) - 8 + (6x) =$

## Solving Equations

Evaluate each expression when: x = 2

**1)** $5x - 10 + 2x =$

**2)** $9 + \dfrac{x}{2} =$

**3)** $5x + 7 =$

**4)** $5 - x =$

**5)** $4 \div x =$

**6)** $7 \div (x + 3) =$

**7)** $6x + 7 =$

**8)** $6 + 6x =$

**9)** $10 + (10x + 4) =$

**10)** $10x - x =$

<u>**Find Numbers (Verbal Algebra)**</u>

Verbal algebra involves translating word problems or verbal statements into algebraic expressions or equations.

For example: The product of the two numbers is 91. One number is six less than the other. What are the numbers?

We're given a verbal description of a problem, and we need to represent it using algebraic symbols and equations.

Let's break down the given problem into algebraic expressions:

- Given that the product of the two numbers is 91, we can write the equation: $xy = 91$
- Also, given that one number is six less than the other, we can write another equation: $x = y - 6$

Now, we can use algebraic techniques to solve the system of equations to find the values of $x$ and $y$, which represent the two numbers.

$$x(x - 6) = 91$$

1. **Solve the equation:**

   - Expand the equation:

   $$x^2 - 6x = 91$$

   - Rearrange the equation into standard quadratic form:

   $$x^2 - 6x - 91 = 0$$

   - Factor the quadratic equation:

   $$(x - 13)(x + 7) = 0$$

2. **Find the solutions for $x$:**

   - From the factored form, we have two possible values for $x$:

$$x = 13 \text{ or } x = -7$$

3. **Check the validity of the solutions:**

   - Since one number is six less than the other, we discard the negative solution.

   - Therefore, the solution is $x = 13$.

4. **Find the other number:**

   - Substitute $x = 13$ into the expression for the other number:

   Other number $= x - 6 = 13 - 6 = 7$

So, the two numbers are 13 and 7.

## Verbal Algebra

1) A number increased by eight is 17. Find the number.

2) One number is nine times another. Their sum is 80. Find the numbers.

3) The quotient of a number and three is 7. Find the number.

4) A number diminished by 9 is 4. Find the number.

5) Nine less than a number is 2. Find the number.

**6)** Three less than a number is 3. Find the number.

**7)** Nine less than a number is 3. Find the number.

**8)** Three-fifths of a number is 3. Find the number.

**9)** The product of six and a number is 6. What is the number?

**10)** The product of three and a number is 9. What is the number?

11) When a number is divided by five, the result is 5. What is the number?

12) One number is four times another. Their sum is 25. Find the numbers.

13) Two-fourths of a number is 0. Find the number.

14) The sum of three consecutive numbers is 24. What are the numbers?

15) One less than four times a number is 15. Find the number.

**16)** When a number is divided by eight, the result is 8. What is the number?

**17)** The quotient of a number and seven is 4. Find the number.

**18)** Two-thirds of a number is 2. Find the number.

**19)** One-half of a number is 1. Find the number.

**20)** The quotient of a number and three is 9. Find the number.

**21)** Twice a number is 6. What is the number?

**22)**    Eight less than a number is 6. Find the number.

**23)**    When a number is divided by nine, the result is 1. What is the number?

**24)**    A number diminished by 7 is 7. Find the number.

**25)**    One number is three times another. Their sum is 12. Find the numbers.

<u>**Simplifying Expressions**</u>

It involves combining like terms and performing operations to make the expression easier to understand and work with.

Let's simplify the expression:

$$2x - 2x + 8 + 4$$

- **Combine like terms:** First, we look for terms with the same variable and exponent. In this expression, $2x$ and $-2x$ are like terms, so they can be combined:

$$2x - 2x = 0$$

- **Substitute the simplified terms:** After combining the like terms, the expression becomes:

$$0 + 8 + 4$$

- **Combine the remaining terms:** Now, we add the constants together:

$$8 + 4 = 12$$

## Simplify Expressions

1) $20k - 7 + 9k - 17 + 8k + 3$

2) $-9 + 5 - 15x + 7x - 12 + 14x$

3) $5m - 4m + 12m - 11 + 14$

4) $-18z + 16 - 19 + 4z$

5) $4 - 3(-12k + 14)$

6) $-2z - 14 - z$

7) $12x - 18 + 9x - 13 + 19x + 3$

8) $18 + 3(z - 10)$

9) $x + 14 + 20x$

10) $-15 - 9k + 5k - 3 + 11k$

**11)** $-16 - 15x + 6x - 14 + 5x$

**12)** $11k + k$

**13)** $-z + 14z$

**14)** $7y - 11 + 3y - 6 + 11y + 15$

**15)** $-20 + 13 - 11y + 2y - 15 + 15y$

**16)** $-14m + 10m$

**17)** $12k - 6k + 10 + 19$

**18)** $-12k + 17 - 5 + 9k$

**19)** $4z - 15 - 13z + 12$

**20)** $13 + 7(18y - 18)$

**21)** $12z + 4z$

**22)** $14k - 12 - 12k + 11$

**23)** $-14z + 15 + 12z + 18 + 16z - 19$

**24)** $18k + 4 + 8k$

**25)** $-2x + 6 - x$

**26)** $y + 12 + 2y$

**27)** $19 + 19 + 9z - 9z + 17 - 19z$

**28)** $-19y - 18 - 5 - 12y$

**29)** $19 + 7x - 20 + 3x$

**30)** $6z - 12 - z + 19$

**31)** $-14 + 14y + 3 - 10y$

**32)** $-15z - 6z$

**33)** $15 + 2y - 11 + 14y - 14 + 3y$

**34)** $5 + y - 19 + 14y$

**35)** $20 + 17y - 13y$

**36)** $z + 6 + 2z$

**37)** $-3z + 4 + 15z$

**38)** $-9 - 20z + 20 - 5z$

**39)** $15m + 6 + 7m + 5 + 2m + 13$

**40)** $3 + 4z - 9z + 14 - 7z$

**41)** $18y + 16 - 16y + 19 + 2y + 2$

**42)** $13 - 2(13x - 9)$

**43)** $-12x - 3 - 20x$

**44)** $-13x - 10x$

**45)** $-x - 9x$

**46)** $-9 - 2y + 12y - 10 + 19y$

**47)** $-5z + 9z$

**48)** $5z + 8 + 16z + 4 + 6z + 20$

**49)** $-14k + 20 + 18k + 13 + 13k - 11$

**50)** $-9 - 19k + 6 - 11k$

## Linear Functions

A linear equation is an algebraic equation that represents a straight line when graphed on a coordinate plane. It consists of variables raised to the power of 1 (i.e., no exponents higher than 1) and constant coefficients.

The general form of a linear equation in one variable x is:

$$ax + b = 0$$

Where $a$ and $b$ are constants, and $x$ is the variable.

Let's solve the linear equation:

$$-2x + 9 = 5$$

- **Isolate the variable term:** We want to isolate the term containing $x$ on one side of the equation. To do this, we'll move the constant term to the other side. Subtract 9 from both sides:

$$-2x + 9 - 9 = 5 - 9$$

$$-2x = -4$$

- **Divide by the coefficient of the variable:** To solve for $x$, divide both sides by the coefficient of $x$, which is -2:

$$\frac{-2x}{-2} = \frac{-4}{-2}$$

$$x = 2$$

## Linear Equations

Solve for the variable.

**1)** $9(-10y - (-2)) = -342$

**2)** $-7y + (-2) = 68$

**3)** $-2y + (-5)y - (-8) = -41$

**4)** $6x = 12$

**5)** $-6x + (-6)x = -84$

**6)** $9x + (-2)x = -35$

**7)** $9y + (-10) = -55$

**8)** $4y + (-9) = -21$

**9)** $-4x + 4 = 8$

**10)** $-8y + (-10) = -18$

**11)** $-3y - (-7) = 1$

**12)** $8y + (-5) = 67$

**13)** $6x + 7 = -53$

**14)** $10x = -40$

**15)** $-3y + (-7) = -4$

**16)** $8x = 32$

**17)** $9y + (-5)y - 5 = -29$

**18)** $-8(-5y - (-7)) = -336$

**19)** $8x + (-4)x = -16$

**20)** $-3x + 1 = -20$

**21)** $5x + (-4) = -24$

**22)** $-5x + (-7) = -32$

**23)** $-1y + 8y - 10 = -38$

**24)** $-7x + x = 30$

## Slop from Two Points

The slope between two points on a Cartesian coordinate system is a measure of the steepness of the line connecting those points. It's calculated by finding the change in the y-coordinates divided by the change in the x-coordinates.

- The coordinates of the first point as $(x1 , y1) = ( 2, -30)$.

- The coordinates of the second point as $(x2 , y2) = (-5, 40)$.

The formula to calculate the slope ($m$) between two points:

$$\frac{y2 - y1}{x2 - x1}$$

## Find Slope from two Points

**1)** (-13, -2 ) and (9 , -9 )

**2)** (5, -8 ) and (-7 , 3 )

**3)** (14, 7 ) and (-12 , -12 )

**4)** (-14, -17 ) and (-16 , -13 )

**5)** (-12, -19 ) and (-9 , 0 )

**6)** (-1, -7 ) and (5 , 10 )

**7)** (-2, -9 ) and (-8 , 20 )

**8)** (10, -17 ) and (-9 , 10 )

**9)** (20, 6 ) and (-18 , 10 )

**10)** (-3, -6 ) and (17 , -14 )

**11)** (0, -10 ) and (-18 , -2 )

**12)** (-12, 11 ) and (15 , 1 )

**13)** (15, -10 ) and (19 , -10 )

**14)** (18, -1 ) and (3 , 14 )

**15)** (14, 19 ) and (13 , -6 )

**16)** (20, -7 ) and (14 , 11 )

**17)** (-5, -1 ) and (-12 , 1 )

**18)** (-20, -5 ) and (10 , 14 )

**19)** (-16, -16 ) and (20 , -11 )

**20)** (-10, -14 ) and (2 , 8 )

**21)** (-4, 12 ) and (-15 , -1 )

**22)** (-16, -19 ) and (12 , 1 )

**23)** (-17, -12 ) and (17 , -2 )

**24)** (2, 3 ) and (-13 , -14 )

## Graphing Linear Equation

Graphing a linear equation involves plotting the points that satisfy the equation on a coordinate plane and connecting them to form a straight line. Linear equations are equations of the form $y = mx + b$, where $m$ represents the slope of the line, and $b$ represents the y-intercept, the point where the line intersects the y-axis.

To graph a linear equation:

1. Identify the slope ($m$) and y-intercept ($b$) from the equation.

2. Plot the y-intercept $(0,b)$) as a point on the y-axis.

3. Use the slope to find additional points on the line. The slope represents the change in y for every unit change in x.

4. Connect the points to form a straight line.

For example, to graph the equation:

$$y = \frac{9}{4}x - 8$$

1. **Identify the slope and y-intercept:** The slope is $\frac{9}{4}$, and the y-intercept is −8.

2. **Plot the y-intercept:** Plot the point $(0,-8)$.

3. **Use the slope to plot additional points:** the slop is $\frac{9}{4}$ to find another point. we will move up 9 units and 4 units to the right from the y-intercept to find another point.

4. **Draw the line:** Once we have at least two points, we can draw a straight line.

We can continue this process to plot more points and extend the line further if needed.

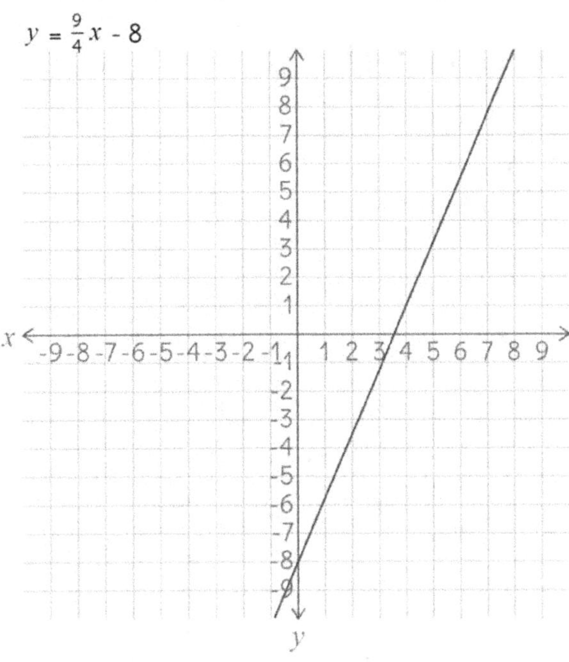

## Graphing Linear Equations

**1)**  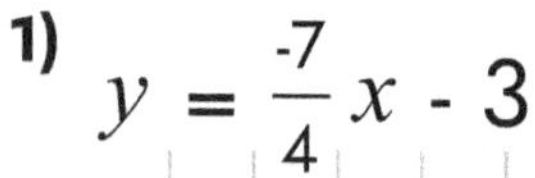

$$y = \frac{-7}{4}x - 3$$

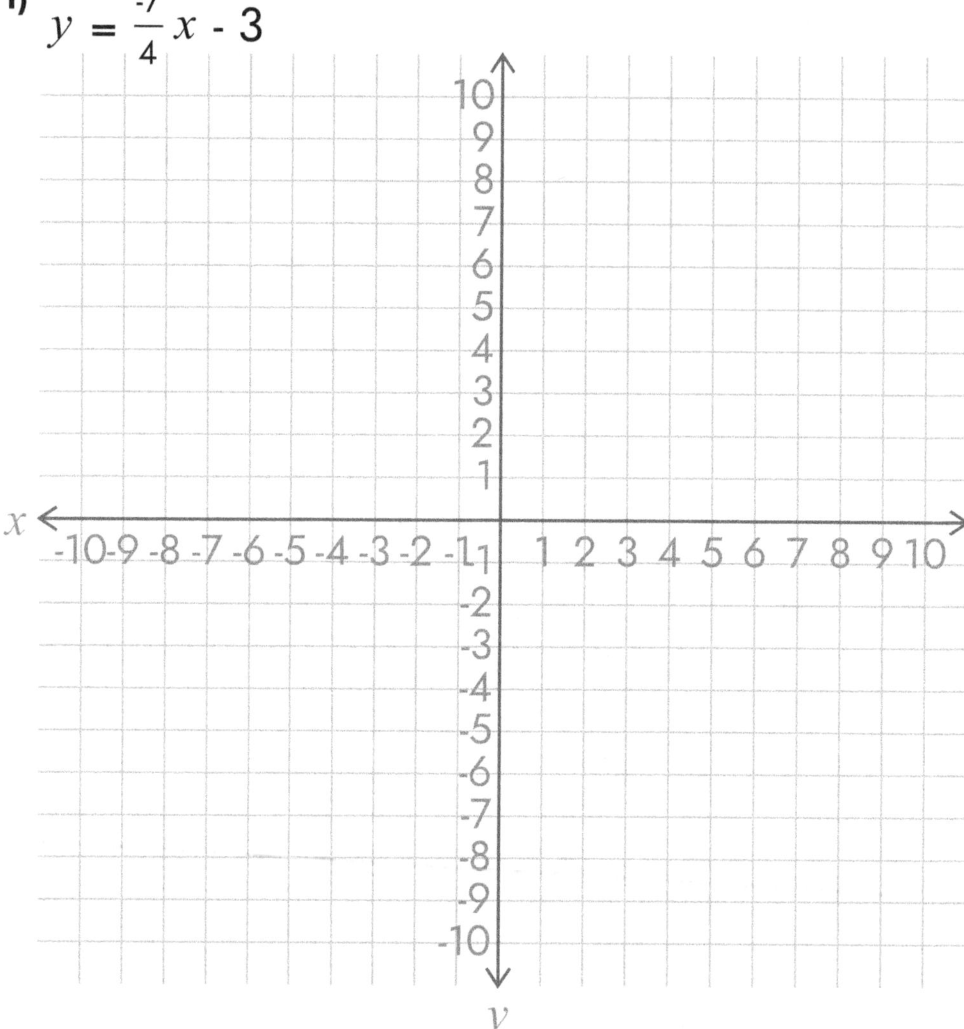

**2)**

$$y = \frac{5}{4}x - 3$$

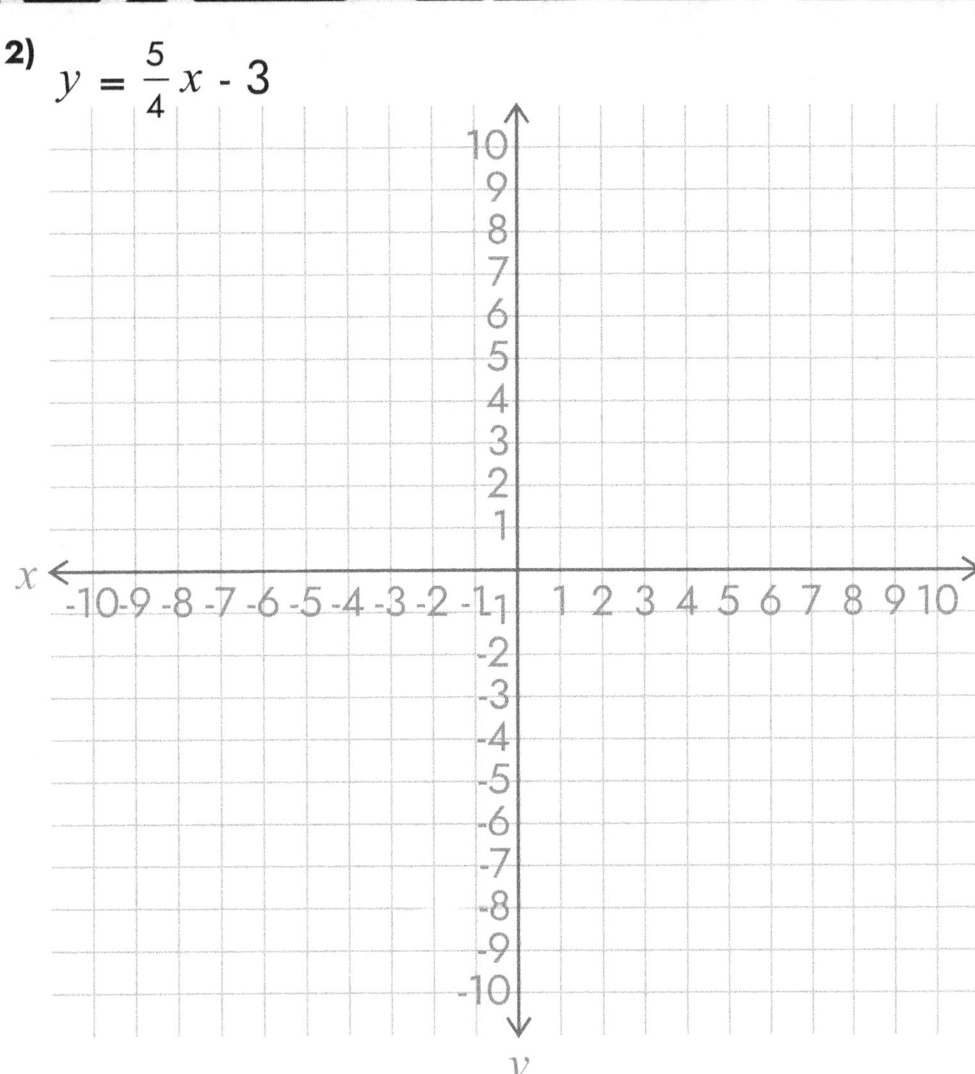

**3)**

$$y = \frac{5}{4}x + 4$$

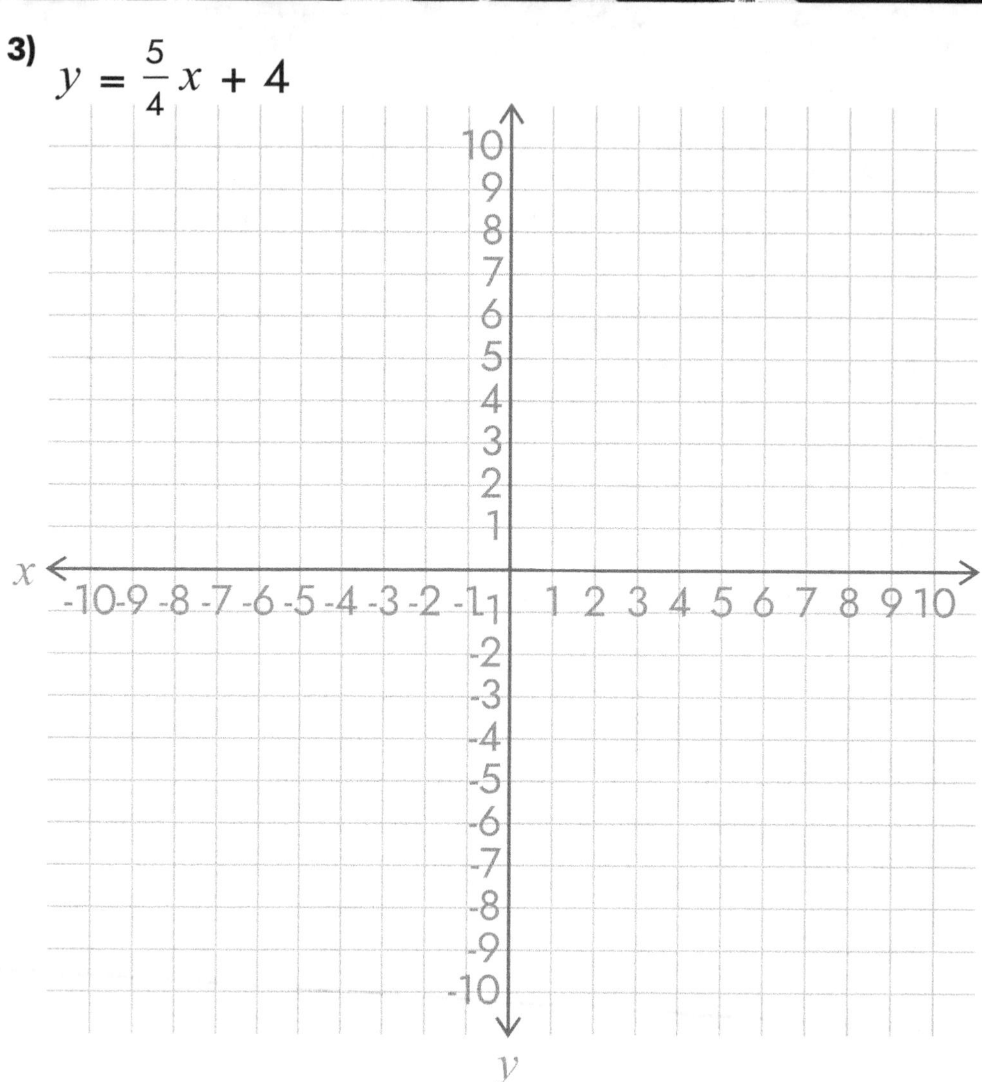

**4)** $y = \dfrac{-1}{4}x + 6$

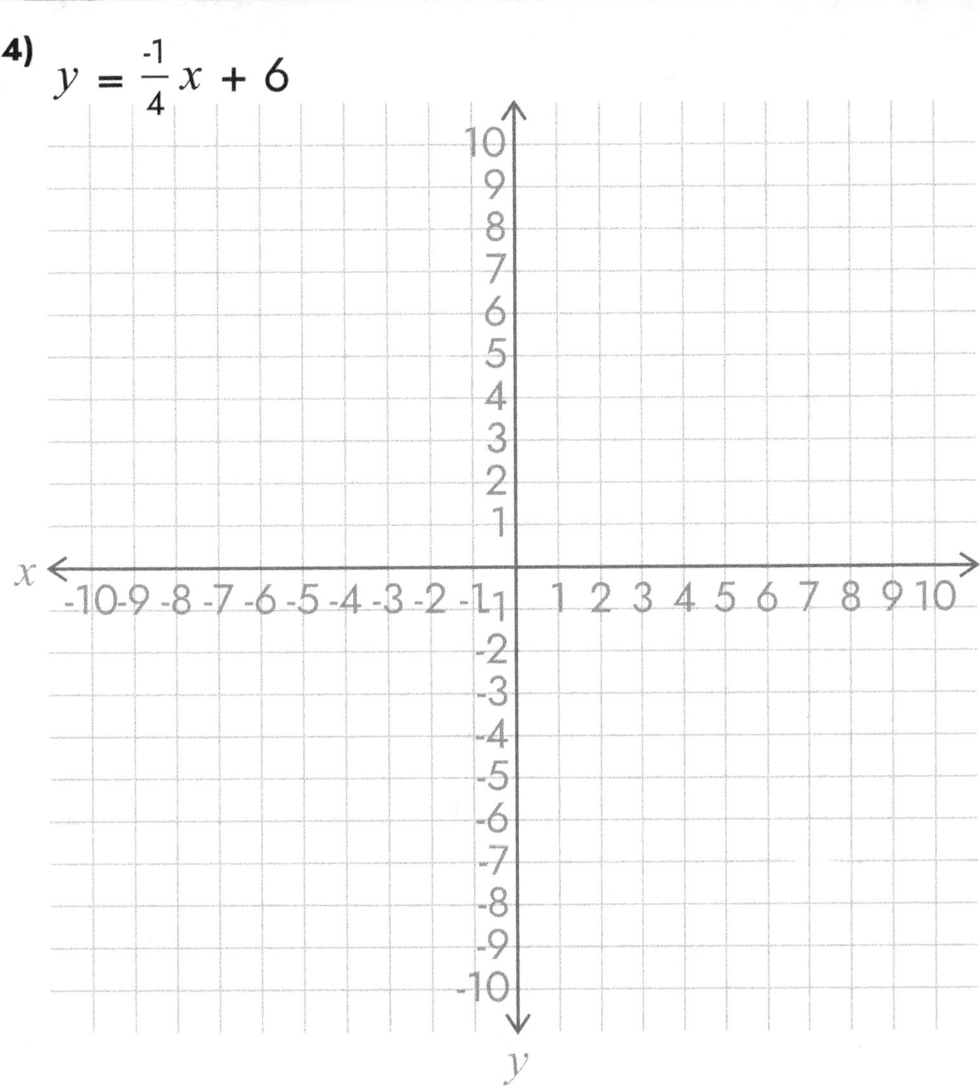

SUMMER MATH WORKBOOK
NAME:
BUILDING ACTIVITIES

**5)**

$$y = \frac{-1}{4}x - 5$$

x
y
-10 -9 -8 -7 -6 -5 -4 -3 -2 -1
1 2 3 4 5 6 7 8 9 10
10 9 8 7 6 5 4 3 2 1
-2 -3 -4 -5 -6 -7 -8 -9 -10

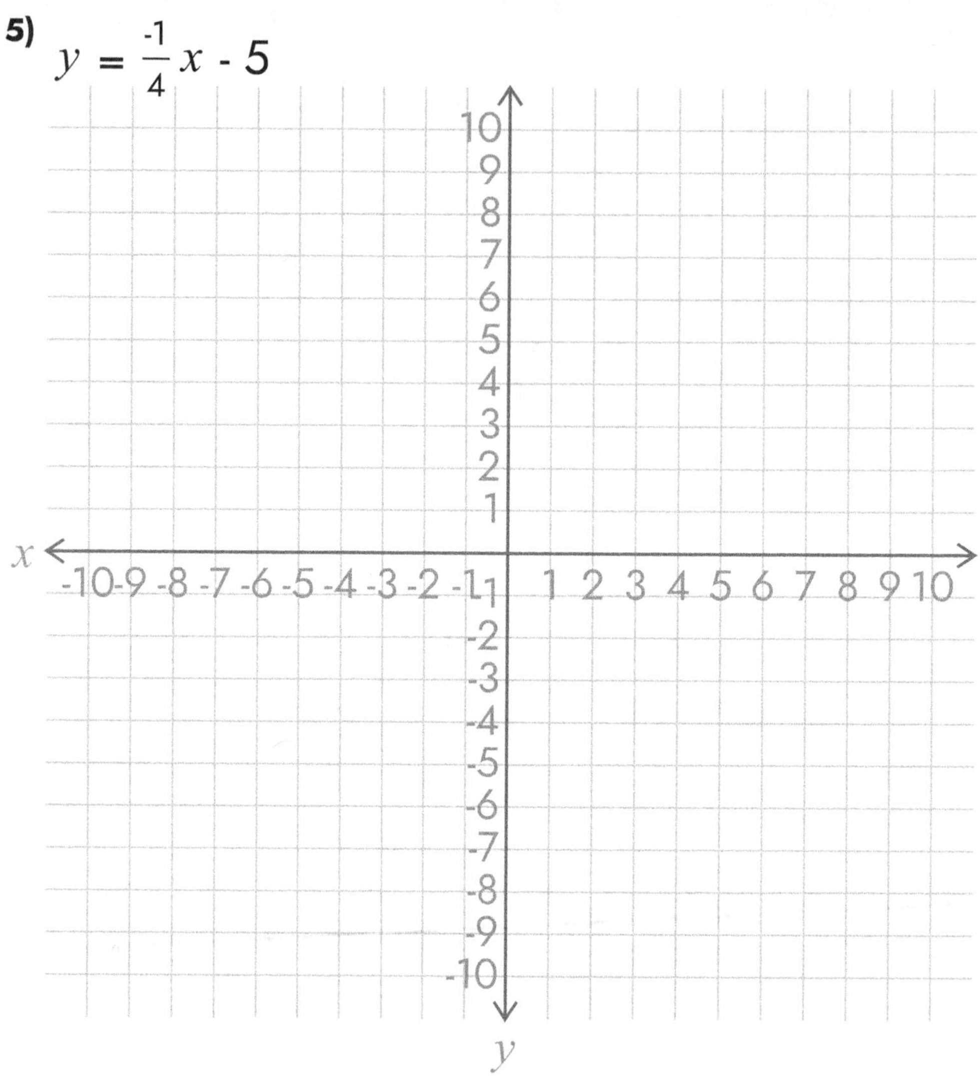

# ANSWERS

**Page 1:  Equations (One Side)**

1. $x = 7$  2. $y = 5$  3. $z = 5$  4. $y = 7$  5. $y = 9$  6. $y = 6$

7. $y = 9$  8. $z = 1$  9. $k = 7$  10. $z = 2$  11. $x = 4$  12. $y = 16$

13. $y = 2$  14. $z = 3$  15. $m = 1$  16. $z = 9$  17. $m = 10$  18. $y = 1$

19. $x = 2$  20. $m = 8$  21. $x = 7$  22. $m = 9$  23. $x = 9$  24. $k = 5$

25. $y = 1$  26. $x = 9$  27. $y = 8$  28. $z = 4$  29. $y = 2$  30. $y = 6$

31. $z = 10$  32. $m = 8$  33. $k = 1$  34. $k = 3$  35. $m = 6$  36. $m = 7$

37. $y = 1$  38. $y = 10$  39. $k = 3$  40. $z = 3$  41. $k = 2$  42. $x = 2$

43. $k = 8$  44. $m = 24$  45. $m = 7$  46. $y = 8$  47. $y = 7$  48. $z = 7$

49. $m = 1$  50. $z = 4$  51. $y = 7$  52. $y = 9$  53. $k = 9$  54. $m = 7$

55. $y = 10$  56. $k = 5$  57. $m = 9$  58. $z = 5$  59. $z = 2$  60. $m = 5$

61. $z = 5$  62. $z = 8$  63. $k = 3$  64. $x = 3$  65. $k = 56$  66. $m = 20$

67. $x = 8$  68. $x = 10$  69. $x = 5$  70. $z = 6$

**Page 8:  Equations (Two Sides)**

1. $x = 8$  2. $y = 7$  3. $z = 4$  4. $z = 6$  5. $k = 8$  6. $m = 8$  7. $z = 1$

8. $z = 7$  9. $y = 3$  10. $k = 1$  11. $y = 6$  12. $k = 4$  13. $y = 6$  14. $z = 5$

15. $m = 9$  16. $m = 3$  17. $y = 5$  18. $z = 5$  19. $m = 1$  20. $x = 5$  21. $z = 4$

22. $x = 1$  23. $z = 2$  24. $y = 8$  25. $m = 5$  26. $z = 3$  27. $k = 9$  28. $k = 2$

29. $x = 5$  30. $y = 9$  31. $y = 7$  32. $m = 6$  33. $x = 2$  34. $m = 3$  35. $m = 4$

36. $y = 2$  37. $x = 1$  38. $m = 7$  39. $y = 3$  40. $y = 4$  41. $x = 8$  42. $z = 2$

**43.** z = 3     **44.** z = 1     **45.** z = 2     **46.** k = 5     **47.** x = 6     **48.** y = 8     **49.** z = 3

**50.** z = 1     **51.** z = 1     **52.** y = 6     **53.** m = 4     **54.** k = 4     **55.** y = 5     **56.** k = 7

**57.** y = 1     **58.** k = 2     **59.** y = 8     **60.** m = 2     **61.** m = 6     **62.** z = 4     **63.** x = 4

**64.** z = 7     **65.** x = 9     **66.** x = 7     **67.** x = 8     **68.** x = 6     **69.** x = 7     **70.** y = 3

**71.** y = 9     **72.** x = 2     **73.** m = 9     **74.** y = 6     **75.** k = 9     **76.** k = 3     **77.** y = 9

**78.** k = 7

## Page 16:   Order of Operations (PEMDAS)

**1.** -13     **2.** 25     **3.** 24     **4.** 234     **5.** 120     **6.** 1,601     **7.** 80

**8.** 121     **9.** 36     **10.** 24     **11.** 61     **12.** 63     **13.** 326     **14.** 225

**15.** 2     **16.** 15     **17.** 72     **18.** 108     **19.** 252     **20.** 60     **21.** 27

**22.** 71     **23.** 25     **24.** 144     **25.** 17     **26.** 42     **27.** 11     **28.** 4

**29.** 7     **30.** 35     **31.** 36     **32.** 36     **33.** 16     **34.** 69     **35.** 169

**36.** 448     **37.** 108     **38.** 23     **39.** 96     **40.** 30     **41.** 15     **42.** 8

**43.** 4     **44.** 18     **45.** 116     **46.** -7     **47.** 27     **48.** 15     **49.** 26

**50.** 35     **51.** 42     **52.** 18     **53.** 20     **54.** 29     **55.** 5     **56.** 23

**57.** 1,231     **58.** 21     **59.** 14     **60.** 17     **61.** 336     **62.** 3     **63.** 15

**64.** 45     **65.** 7     **66.** 20     **67.** 23     **68.** 64

## Page 23:   Mixed Numbers

**1.** 16 11/12     **2.** 55/96     **3.** 8/9     **4.** 55/56     **5.** 43 7/10

**6.** 11 67/72     **7.** 50/51     **8.** 11/17     **9.** 1 1/61     **10.** 1 1/6

**11.** 13 2/15     **12.** 10 14/15     **13.** 1     **14.** 56 20/21     **15.** 8 7/12

**16.** 12 8/15     **17.** 1 1/5     **18.** 4 3/8     **19.** 1 29/36     **20.** 77 33/35

**Page 27: Solving Inequalities**

| | | | | |
|---|---|---|---|---|
| **1.** $x \geq -1$ | **2.** $y < -63$ | **3.** $m < -1$ | **4.** $m < -3/5$ | **5.** $z \geq -1$ |
| **6.** $x > 13$ | **7.** $z \leq 3/4$ | **8.** $z < 64$ | **9.** $m \leq -1/2$ | **10.** $k > -9$ |
| **11.** $x > 0$ | **12.** $z > -24$ | **13.** $k > 12$ | **14.** $m < -4$ | **15.** $x \geq -3$ |
| **16.** $k < -5/3$ | **17.** $m \geq 20$ | **18.** $k > -2$ | **19.** $y \leq -2$ | **20.** $m \leq 3/2$ |
| **21.** $z \leq -2$ | **22.** $m \leq 1$ | **23.** $y < -1$ | **24.** $y \geq 27$ | **25.** $z \leq 3$ |
| **26.** $m \geq -6$ | **27.** $x < -5/2$ | **28.** $z > -7$ | **29.** $k > -18$ | **30.** $x > -1$ |
| **31.** $x < 5/3$ | **32.** $y \geq -3$ | **33.** $m < -35$ | **34.** $m \leq 15$ | **35.** $x \geq 6$ |
| **36.** $m \geq 2$ | **37.** $x < -14$ | **38.** $m < 6/5$ | **39.** $m \geq 4$ | **40.** $y \geq -16$ |
| **41.** $x \geq 7$ | **42.** $y \leq -3/7$ | **43.** $k \leq 12$ | **44.** $k > 56$ | **45.** $y \geq -6$ |
| **46.** $z \geq 40$ | **47.** $y \geq 13$ | **48.** $x \leq 3/2$ | | |

**Page 39: Solving Equations**

**1.** 10    **2.** 20    **3.** 30    **4.** 10    **5.** 35    **6.** 11    **7.** 37    **8.** -3    **9.** 12    **10.** 9

**Page 40: Solving Equations**

**1.** 63    **2.** 104    **3.** 26    **4.** 33    **5.** 28    **6.** 30    **7.** 1    **8.** 70    **9.** 49

**10.** 65

**Page 41: Solving Equations**

**1.** 700    **2.** 50    **3.** 30    **4.** 85    **5.** 14    **6.** 36    **7.** 20    **8.** 750    **9.** 300

**10.** 11

**Page 42: Solving Equations**

**1.** 17    **2.** 108    **3.** -3    **4.** 57    **5.** 60    **6.** 62    **7.** 23    **8.** 21    **9.** 8

**10.** -1

**Page 43:   Solving Equations**

**1.** 63   **2.** 28   **3.** 12   **4.** 1   **5.** 17   **6.** 63   **7.** 0   **8.** 3   **9.** 188   **10.** 72

**Page 44:   Solving Equations**

**1.** 4   **2.** 10   **3.** 17   **4.** 3   **5.** 2   **6.** 1.4   **7.** 19   **8.** 18   **9.** 34   **10.** 18

**Page 45:   Verbal Algebra**

**1.** 9   **2.** 8, 72   **3.** 21   **4.** 13   **5.** 11   **6.** 6

**7.** 12   **8.** 5   **9.** 1   **10.** 3   **11.** 25   **12.** 5, 20

**13.** 0   **14.** 7, 8, 9   **15.** 4   **16.** 64   **17.** 28   **18.** 3

**19.** 2   **20.** 27   **21.** 3   **22.** 14   **23.** 9   **24.** 14

**25.** 3, 9

**Page 50:   Simplify Expressions**

**1.** $37k - 21$   **2.** $6x - 16$   **3.** $13m + 3$   **4.** $-14z - 3$   **5.** $36k - 38$

**6.** $-3z - 14$   **7.** $40x - 28$   **8.** $3z - 12$   **9.** $21x + 14$   **10.** $7k - 18$

**11.** $-4x - 30$   **12.** $12k$   **13.** $13z$   **14.** $21y - 2$   **15.** $6y - 22$

**16.** $-4m$   **17.** $6k + 29$   **18.** $-3k + 12$   **19.** $-9z - 3$   **20.** $126y - 113$

**21.** $16z$   **22.** $2k - 1$   **23.** $14z + 14$   **24.** $26k + 4$   **25.** $-3x + 6$

**26.** $3y + 12$   **27.** $-19z + 55$   **28.** $-31y - 23$   **29.** $10x - 1$   **30.** $5z + 7$

**31.** $4y - 11$   **32.** $-21z$   **33.** $19y - 10$   **34.** $15y - 14$   **35.** $4y + 20$

**36.** $3z + 6$   **37.** $12z + 4$   **38.** $-25z + 11$   **39.** $24m + 24$   **40.** $-12z + 17$

**41.** $4y + 37$   **42.** $-26x + 31$   **43.** $-32x - 3$   **44.** $-23x$   **45.** $-10x$

**46.** $29y - 19$   **47.** $4z$   **48.** $27z + 32$   **49.** $17k + 22$   **50.** $-30k - 3$